First Printing, 2014

www.AllSapJobs.com

(1) (22) GREAT IDEA

✗✗ (2) SAP TECHNOLOGY (PDF)

(3) 39 (How To Train)

(4) 51 (How To GET JOB)

(TO LEARN)

FAMILIAR WITH THE INTERNET!
click & AD SEE
WHAT POPS UP.
LOOK GOOD AT EVERY
SCREEN AD MAN!

1

Getting started in SAP

How to transform your career and become a highly paid SAP expert

Contents

*JIM STEWART *   SITES   (TO GET INTO SAP)

* (1.) SAPCOOKBOOK. com   (4.)

* (2.) BREAKINGINTOSAP. com   (5.)

(3.)   (6.)

Preface - What's in this Book?

Inside this book you'll find out what SAP software does, what kind of careers there are in the world of SAP, and why a career in SAP might make sense for you. You'll learn about SAP projects and roles and what hiring managers are looking for on resumes and in interviews. You'll learn how to make and execute a plan to get you working with SAP, including how you can overcome the catch-22 of no SAP experience meaning no SAP job. You'll learn how to evaluate the marketplace and your skill set in order to pick a focus area and specialization strategy. You'll learn what to do and what not to do to succeed after you've landed an SAP job, and how to move ahead to the next level if you'd like to become a consultant or independent contractor. Finally, the appendix is a critical reference resource with links to an extensive list of SAP customers, consulting companies, and other potential employers to target in your job search.

This book shares practical advice about how to get started and succeed in a lucrative career working with SAP software. You'll learn what SAP is all about, what kind of jobs there are in the SAP world, and how **you** can get one. If you're already working with SAP, you'll find that this book is a handy reference for furthering your SAP career and navigating the many career options available to you. The book features a step-by-step roadmap for career success and lays out the big picture of the SAP ecosystem so you'll understand where you can fit in.

I've been working in the SAP world for the past seventeen years. Along the way, I have worked in just about every role imaginable: consultant, project manager, consulting manager, consulting sales, solution marketing, consulting director, independent contractor and applications director. My SAP journey started in 1997 when I joined SAP America as an applications consultant. Over the course of following ten years I worked on multiple customer projects, became a manager and then director of the CRM consulting solutions group. I then left SAP in 2006 to start my own SAP consulting business and work as an independent contractor. After six years of contracting work I moved over to the customer side of the SAP world as Director of SAP Applications for a large action sports apparel company in Orange County, California. Consulting work eventually lured me back, and I've been running my own boutique SAP consulting firm ever since.

During my SAP career I've had the opportunity to work on many different SAP implementation projects. I've hired consultants, project managers, programmers, and business analysts. I've been both an interviewer and an interviewee countless times and I've seen what works and what doesn't work in interviews and on resumes. I've had work brought to me by large consulting firms and I've had to chase down my own project opportunities as an independent consultant. I've worked on small projects with a handful of team members and on huge multi-year deployments at Fortune 500 companies where the project teams filled football-field-sized rooms.

Because of the variety and depth of my SAP experience, I'm able to offer you a unique perspective on what you need to know in order to launch and sustain a career in the world of SAP. I certainly wish a guide like this had been available to me seventeen years ago!

Why a Career in SAP?

The last forty years have been a period of tremendous technological change. From the mid-seventies, an age that started with mainframe computers, through the eighties to client server computing to the nineties and the internet revolution, as well as the mobile, social media, and cloud upheaval of the present day, SAP has not only survived, but thrived. In fact, in the large enterprise space for business applications, only SAP and Oracle have come out intact. One-time competitors (Siebel, Arriba, Commerce One, Lawson, Baan, PeopleSoft, and JD Edwards, to name a few) have been acquired or have fallen by the wayside. As any financial prospectus will warn you, past performance is no guarantee for the future, though it's probably the best indicator we have. If you're asking yourself why you should invest your time, energy, and future on SAP products, one compelling reason is that the company has a track record of success. Founded in 1972 by former IBMers (they couldn't get IBM interested in business applications at the time), SAP has been going strong for forty-one years and counting.

Another reason why SAP is a good career choice is what is known as the "installed base," the huge number of companies running SAP software as their primary business application. Over 70 percent of Fortune 100 and 50 percent of Fortune 500 companies run SAP as a core business system. The number of companies running SAP software is over 183,000 in 130 countries. More companies are added to that list every year. See the appendix for a list of those companies. For you, this means that in addition to all the job opportunities involving implementing SAP, there are also jobs at all of the

6

companies with SAP software already installed to help roll out new functionality, upgrade, or just operate their day-to-day business.

We won't spend too much time here on what SAP software does for a business because there are plenty of books and websites where you can read about that in detail. Our focus is on SAP careers. However, you do need to know the basics of SAP. As a package, it's huge: a mile wide and a mile deep with a large breadth of functionality and depth within that functionality. It's also not the most intuitive product to work with, and that's where you, the SAP expert, come in. If you can learn to use, configure, program, administer, or do one of a hundred other things with SAP software, then you are a valuable asset to businesses. People who know SAP are highly compensated for their knowledge, usually at an above-market rate when compared to other software skill sets. This holds true for just about every role in the SAP world, such as business user, business analyst, consultant, and contractor. We'll go further into roles and compensation in later chapters, but for now let's just say that learning SAP is an excellent way to increase both your marketability and your compensation.

Finally, an important aspect of SAP is that it is not static. The company pours a tremendous amount of money into R&D, which often translates into new functionality and new opportunity. If you enjoy learning new things, going new places, and working with new people, then opportunities abound in the SAP market. So let's get started!

What is SAP?

Ok, that's 'S-A-P', not 'SAP' as in tree sap. You will hear it said both ways but if you want to hang out with the cool kids it's 'S-A-P'. Got it? Ok, you're halfway to a career in SAP! I'm only half kidding because one of the first things you should learn about SAP is that it is a truly an acronym soup and full of jargon. Some have called this collection of terms 'Sapanese' because to an outside ear it can sound like a foreign language. To make it in the SAP world you'll have to learn this language. Your fluency, or lack thereof, will signal your knowledge and expertise to others. We'll cover more on this later as well as in the appendix.

In a nutshell SAP software is an integrated package of business applications. From a business point of view SAP allows salespeople to enter orders for customers, purchasing to buy products from vendors, production people to build things, the warehouse to ship, and finance to keep the books. It can do all this in multiple languages across multiple currencies meeting various legal requirements for business around the world. The SAP core product (R/3 originally, now called ECC) was built organically from the ground up and it has a tight integration that is one the key value propositions of the product suite. Everything in SAP is tied together in one common data dictionary across all areas. The look and feel of the screens are also common across all business areas. This kind of approach is in contrast to the other big dog of ERP (Enterprise Resource Planning), Oracle, which grew many of its business application functionality by buying other software companies and tying them together. In the last few years SAP has gone on its own buying spree acquiring the likes of

Business Objects, SuccessFactors, Ariba, and Hybris, but the core functionality was all built in-house at SAP.

At some point most companies go through a make or buy decision when selecting the software that they are going to use to run their business. If they choose to buy software rather than build it themselves then they would typically select a "packaged application" which means pre-built software which could (theoretically) run off the shelf as is; just like you would buy a box containing Office (at least in the old days you would buy a box). The basic idea around buying a packaged application is that you believe that a software company is better suited to building business software for you than you are building it yourself. After all, the reasoning goes, a software company should be better at building software than an oil company or a shoe business. A software vendor can also offer a much better solution in terms of ongoing support, stability, and functionality. SAP software comes with a huge set of best practice business processes already built into the package. Additionally with a package one has the comfort that the software has been proven to work across thousands of other companies. The converse argument is that nobody knows how our business works better than us. Or that our business is so different that no packaged application can work exactly the way we want it to. The downside of a packaged application is that it is not going to come customized to work exactly the way a given company might want it to. That's why SAP software is built with various methods for customizing it so that it can come closer to working exactly how a given company wants it to while still maintaining the same stability and flexibility that make it attractive in the first place.

THIS

X The first method of this customization is called configuration. SAP has a specific transaction (SPRO) with a menu tree built into it, offering the ability to customize the flow and functionality of various business processes. I've heard it described as a set of switches and tables for changing SAP functionality, but that description must have been thought up by someone who hasn't really worked with the software. The SPRO transaction takes the user into what is called the IMG (implementation guide), which is a menu path organized by functional area.

The IMG allows the consultant or business analyst to perform thousands of tasks, such as setting up the company's organizational structure, defining different types of sales orders, and setting up the views of a vendor master record.

The IMG is where business analysts and consultants do much of their work (we'll talk about these job roles in detail in another chapter). Once they understand the business requirements, they bring those requirements to life in the system via configuration. There is a limit to what can be achieved through configuration, however. If the company has a special process that can't be handled though "config," it has to be done through programming (ABAP coding) by the technical consultant. It's worth noting that before any coding is done there should always be a functional specification (spec) written by the analyst or the consultant. After the coding is complete, it should be tested by a functional consultant or analyst to ensure that it meets the business requirement.

There are plenty of other resources that provide more information on what SAP software is all about and what it can do. I've listed several in the appendix if you want to explore the topic further.

10

Orienting Yourself in the World of SAP Careers

Before you can get a job in the SAP field, you need to understand what kind of jobs are out there. You also need to have an understanding of the SAP Ecosystem, the customers and vendors that have a relationship with SAP. At the center of the SAP universe are customers; these are the companies that have purchased SAP software and are either "live" (using the software) or have projects underway to get them live. BMW, Disney, and Apple are a few examples of SAP customers. Even after a company goes live, there is always new functionality, upgrades, or changes that necessitate project work as well as day-to-day production support.

Around the customers swirl the providers of software and services; these are the companies that provide complementary software or consulting services to customers. Accenture, Cap Gemini, and Deloitte Consulting are a few large companies that offer consulting services to companies implementing SAP. The appendix lists some of these service providers. Many other companies offer complementary software that works with SAP software to extend functionality even further. For example, Vistex provides software for sales commissions and rebates, and Win Shuttle offers an Excel interface. SAP publishes a full and lengthy list of certified software partners. As you might expect, there is a lot of moving around in this ecosystem. Consultants leave to join customers, customers leave to become consultants, and so on.

Types of Jobs

Within the SAP Ecosystem there are generally two kinds of roles: functional and technical. As you start out, you'll need to choose an area to focus on in order to move your career forward.

SAP Functional

An SAP functional person is just what it sounds like: someone who understands the *business functions* of SAP software. This is sometimes referred to as someone with applications expertise. These folks understand, for example, the business flow of order to cash and procure to pay, as well as the SAP documents that support that flow. Because SAP is a mile wide and a mile deep, an SAP functional person usually focuses on one SAP module, also known as a functional area. Examples of SAP modules are Sales and Distribution (SD), Materials Management (MM), Finance (FI), and Production Planning (PP). You'll also hear these business functions described as acronyms for their flows. For example, SD aligns with OTC (Order to Cash) process flow and P2P (Procure to Pay) aligns with MM. There are also many other areas and functions in SAP that have grown out of these core modules and are closely related to them. For example, SD and CRM (Customer Relationship Management) go together in terms of process, solution, and skill set because they are both customer oriented. Likewise, MM and APO (Advance Planning and Optimization) are both focused on optimizing the supply chain. In fact, many of the three-letter acronym solutions are extensions of their core brethren. For example, SD has many CRM functionalities built into it, such as order management, pricing, and quotations. However, SD doesn't have other CRM functionality such as opportunity management and sales force automation (SFA), so CRM was introduced as an extension of the core functionality of SD.

A further dimension of the functional world is industry, both in the sense of industry-specific knowledge and as different flavors of SAP software called "Industry Specific Solutions (IS)." In addition to the core SAP software (often called ECC, short for enterprise core component), there are a number of Industry Solutions (IS) that comprise different versions of the software. For example, there is IS-U for utilities, IS-AFS for apparel and footwear, and IS-M for media companies. Functional people with specific expertise in these industry solutions are sometimes in short supply, allowing them to command premium rates. But as with any niche skill, there are fewer companies that have these versions, so the market is smaller than with the generic versions of SAP software.

SAP Technical

SAP technical resources fall into two camps. The first is development, which means programming, usually using ABAP, SAP's core programming language. There are some web-focused areas where Java can be used, but the bread-and-butter programming language of the SAP world is ABAP.

The second technical camp is system administration also called "basis." The folks who work in this camp install the SAP software, monitor the systems, create new clients, and handle performance tuning, among a whole host of other activities.

There is also the area of security and authorizations, which is its own specialty within basis. This area is concerned with user authorizations, the creation of roles, profiles, and security. Security folks are usually specialized and focus solely on security. This is a quasi-technical area, though you don't necessarily need to have a technical background to enter it.

SAP Roles

End User - An end user is someone who uses SAP software on a regular basis as part of their day-to-day job at a company running SAP. This can be a customer service rep entering sales orders, a finance person making journal entries, or an operations person confirming production orders. These people use SAP software as it has been configured and implemented for their company to (hopefully) efficiently and accurately do what they need to do to keep their company running. As with any of these roles, the skill level of individual end users can vary quite a bit, with some simply entering very basic information into screens while others interact with the software and use it intelligently to optimize processes. For example, some CSRs (customer service reps) may simply take a sales order, enter the customer, products, and quantities, and save, whereas others might dig into the ATP (available to promise) details and optimize when and where the customer's products are coming from.

An end user position is an excellent way to gain a foothold in the SAP world because it gets you experience working with SAP software and, more importantly, gets *SAP experience* on your resume. On the many SAP projects I have worked on, I have never failed to be amazed by the people who invariably complain about how awful it is that they have to learn this new "SAP software" when everything was fine and dandy with their old homegrown system. They sometimes have to be dragged kicking and screaming to learn this new and highly transferable skill set. They don't seem to understand that in learning SAP, they gain a skill that is valued by hundreds of thousands of other companies. Change is often hard.

Super User - A super user is an end user who has dove in and learned more than the bare minimum they need to do their daily job. This is someone who one way or another has become the go-to person in their department for others who have questions about or issues with using SAP. They may be officially recognized a super user in their company's support structure or they may just unofficially be the person people know to ask when they're having an issue. They are the next step up in the value chain of human knowledge capital (to throw in a few overused terms of business speak).

The compensation of end users and super users typically has much more to do with their business function and experience than with their SAP knowledge. The important thing for you to know is that these are excellent first steps toward getting the *experience* necessary to move into the SAP world.

SAP Business Analyst - An SAP business analyst serves as an internal consultant to a company. They are expected to have detailed system knowledge and functional expertise in order to support current processes (Production Support) and participate in new deployments of functionality or business units. The business analyst is expected to have both a basic knowledge of business processes and configuration skills in order to customize SAP to meet the needs of the business (i.e., requirements). In order to get hired, a business analyst typically needs to have existing expertise in a certain SAP module. A business analyst will need to have at least a couple of years of SAP experience in order to get the job. We'll talk more about what kind of experience a hiring manager looks for in this role, but you can't be totally green and expect to be hired. Salaries for SAP business analysts typically range from $60,000 to $150,000 a year, depending on the company, location, and candidate's experience. More salary info can be found in the appendix and here: http://www.glassdoor.com/Salaries/sap-business-analyst-salary-SRCH_KO0,20.htm

Consultants - These are the folks that (theoretically, at least) have expert level knowledge of SAP software and the know-how to help companies implement SAP successfully. As with anything else, there is a wide range of skill levels in the consulting realm, from the very green (i.e., just off the school bus) to the very senior (twenty years+) expert level. There is also a wide variety of companies that consultants work for, including "Big 4" consulting firms such as Accenture, SAP's own professional services, Indian companies like Wipro and L&T, small boutique firms, and independent contractors. Consulting firms can be a great way to start your SAP career because they often provide ongoing training, access to early software releases, and a network of skilled colleagues to learn from. But it can be hard to get your foot in the door without SAP experience, and they usually expect full-time travel from their employees. But the pay is good and the variety of project experience can keep things interesting.

Planning an SAP Career

One of the first things you'll need to decide is where you want to play in this SAP universe. To make an informed decision you should consider your background as well as what you want to do. You need to consider the SAP market, which businesses are willing to pay for a given skill set, and your own interests. There's no sense in preparing yourself for an area that has very little demand, nor is there much sense in pushing yourself into an area you dislike.

If you are new to SAP, the good news is that you are a clean slate. You can decide where you want to go and what to focus on. The bad news is that no one is going to hire you. This is one of the conundrums the SAP world shares with many other careers. No one wants to hire someone without experience, but you can't get experience until you are hired. Don't despair, though, because there are ways around this, and everyone working in SAP today has faced and overcome similar challenges. We all have to start somewhere.

If you are new to SAP, you should first take a look at your experience. If you've never had any kind of job before, you first need to get yourself ANY kind of job. Someone with no work experience raises a red flag for any hiring manager. Most businesses are not going to throw someone totally green into an SAP role. SAP is a mission-critical application, and before handing over the keys to the car they are going to want to know that you have at least driven before.

If you are fresh out of college with a computer science degree, you may need to get yourself a programming job using a different language before you can land one doing ABAP, not because ABAP is more complex (it's not), but rather because most companies are risk averse and taking a chance on a totally green candidate is more of an exception than the norm.

Assuming you have some kind of work experience and educational background, think about how you can market yourself. Getting a job is all about marketing and selling yourself; you need to convince

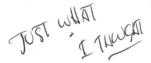

people that you can do the job, that you are not an unpleasant person, and that a company is not going to look like a fool for hiring you. Do you have programming experience or training? That's a natural fit to sell yourself into a technical role. ABAP has similar syntax to COBOL, and someone who knows how to code in another language can pick it up at a basic level pretty quickly. Do you have business process experience? Maybe you worked as a customer service representative. You understand the concept of a sales order header and line items (God knows I didn't when I started out). Maybe you worked in a warehouse and understand the concepts of storing products and bins, packing, and receiving. That's a start on the road to becoming a functional analyst. Maybe you don't have any of these experiences, but you can get them. Regardless, we need to get something on your resume that shows experience. We'll devise a specific plan for this later.

Your calling card is your resume (or CV). Your resume needs to convince people that they should make a small investment of their time in talking to you. SAP is a competitive market, and every open position is likely to have many applicants. The hiring process often starts with a weeding out of resumes; one in which a hundred resumes may be received and only ten deemed worthy of reply. This isn't always the case (sometimes speed of response plays a critical role), but without a decent resume you are dead in the water.

The SAP Marketplace

The second thing to consider is the market for SAP services. What's hot and what's not? Where does demand outstrip supply and vice versa? The technology market is dynamic, so things will change, but here's what I can tell you as of 2014 in the US marketplace. First of all, just as in any market, the marketplace for SAP services (people) is driven by supply and demand. When demand outstrips supply, prices rise; conversely, when there are more people than jobs available, prices (rates and salaries) fall. However, since we are dealing with people and not widgets, the picture is more complicated than it might seem.

SAP is not a monolithic skill set. As has been mentioned, the product is at least a mile wide and a mile deep, and it is constantly changing as new products and functionalities are developed by SAP and by partner companies. This means that there is always something new to learn in the SAP area, and there are always areas with very few knowledgeable people. There are also some very established "classic areas," such as the core modules of SD, MM, FI and PP. All of these have been around since the beginning of SAP, and as a result there are a lot more people who know these areas, some with 20+ years' experience.

This is not the case for newer product areas. The name for the large suite of products released around 2000 was "new dimension" (not so new now); things like CRM, BW, and APO were extensions of classic SAP into growth areas such as SFA, data warehousing, and advanced planning. As a result of these later developments, there are a lot fewer people with ten years of SAP CRM experience than with ten years of SD, for example, and even then, the CRM product has changed tremendously since its inception. There are also a number of niches that haven't been around long or haven't had much traction in the market until recently. As a result, there is less competition in these areas. The same goes for ABAP and basis; these have been around for a long time, so the talent pool is deeper than in some of the newer areas such as web dynpro.

Why should you care about this? Because you need to differentiate yourself from the thousands of people trying to land an SAP job, and one way to do so very nicely is to have a skill set that few others have. SNC anyone?

Finally, at a high level, functional roles tend to pay better than technical ones. This is because of the supply side of things. India tends to churn out a lot more ABAPers than functional consultants. Additionally, folks from non-English-speaking countries gravitate toward programming because there is less emphasis on the advanced communication skills that are necessary in a functional role working with business people in the US. Another thing to keep in mind is the relative maturity of the SAP market across different global geographies. Because it started in Germany, SAP has been around longer in Europe than the US, and longer in the US than in India. This means that there a lot more Europeans who have twenty years of SAP experience than there are Indians with that level of experience. On the other hand, years of experience is just one of the factors that employers look at when hiring.

It's worth noting that India continues to be a hotbed in terms of SAP talent. The word is definitely out in India that SAP is a lucrative skill to have, and there are thousands of young grads who make their way to the US and Europe looking for SAP work. In the US, these folks are typically on sponsored visa programs, so they aren't able to work independently and are usually sponsored by a consulting or customer company.

Specialization vs Generalization

As I've said before, SAP is a mile wide and a mile deep, and there are a few different possible approaches to becoming the most marketable SAP professional you can be. Something to consider is whether you are going to be more of a specialist or a generalist. In the functional realm, you may choose to focus your training, learning, and experience on a well-established module such as SD, which has been around from day one. The good news with this approach is that there is always a good deal of demand out there for essential core modules like SD, MM, and FI. We used to include PP (Production Planning) on this list, but as manufacturing declines in the US, so has the need for PP. The bad news is that if you are just getting into SD, there are a lot of people out there who have been doing it a lot longer than you have. The bottom line is that there is more competition in the established areas. This means you will need to be more creative in differentiating yourself, which you may choose to do by focusing on a particular area of SD such as ATP or Pricing.

A different approach is to specialize. For example, you could specialize in a less popular module (such as SM, QM, or PM), in a newer area (such as HANA or CRM IC Web Channel), or in an industry solution (such as Intellectual Property Management, Lease and Finance, Apparel and Footwear, etc.).

The good thing about specialization is that there are relatively fewer people who will actually have deep expertise, though there are plenty more who will lie about it. The bad thing is that there are typically fewer projects and companies utilizing these more specialized functionalities. Another approach to specialization is to get expertise in one of the many "bolt on" products for SAP (Vertex, Vendavo, and

Vistex to name a few that start with "V"). See the partner link in the appendix for more on these.

The ideal situation is to specialize in an area that has just gotten hot. If you get yourself some experience in a specialty just before that area reaches critical mass, you will be in an excellent place to write your own ticket. Vistex is an add-on product I have seen this happen with lately. Experienced Vistex resources are in high demand because demand is currently outstripping supply, and as a result it's a seller's market—the consultant has their choice of project and can command a higher rate. Employers will also require less experience in these areas because they will not be able to find candidates that have multiple years' experience.

One potential downside of the specialization approach is more travel. Because there are fewer projects in a given specialty, the chance that one is going to pop up in your hometown is considerably lower than with the core areas. If you are going with that approach, you need to be ready to pack your bags and hop on a plane. What I've found to be a nice strategy is to take a dual approach. I have a very solid base in the core SD area, but I also have expertise in the more niche areas of Service Management and CRM Internet Sales and Payment Card processing. As you grow your skill, you will have more options for project selection and location.

If you already have expertise, experience, or interest in a certain industry, it may be a natural fit for you to focus on an industry solution.

Skill Sets (Hard and Soft)

There are two critical skill sets that every SAP knowledge worker needs to have: technical skills, the level of expertise they have with SAP software, and soft skills, how well they can communicate what they are doing, how well they get along with other people, how well they work within a team, etc. Both are vitally important, and the lack of one or the other is often the difference between success and failure in getting or keeping a desired job. In my long SAP career I have come across every kind of mix of these two skill sets. I remember a very bright, highly technical woman who was so unpleasant to work with that everyone avoided talking to her at all costs. She built her own little cube out of foam core when everyone else worked at long open tables. She was eventually fired when it became clear to management that despite her technical expertise she was a project liability because of her inability to work with others. SAP is a team sport! On the other end, I can't forget the garrulous Englishman who never stopped talking and socializing but would always push his responsibilities off to someone else when it came to actually doing work. We referred to him as Mr. Z Table because the only thing he knew how to do with a business requirement was spout off about how it could be built with a "Zed table"; he could rarely leverage the standard SAP pre-built functionality (note to the rest of the world: in America, the letter "Z" is pronounced "Zee" not "Zed"). Most people fall somewhere in between the two extremes, but you should be absolutely clear on the fact that you will be severely hampered in your success if you are strictly a heads-down technologist. Conversely, being all sizzle and no steak will also catch up with you eventually. Both skill sets are critical to have if you're going to convince people that you know what you're doing (and that is more than half the battle in both getting and keeping a job). Another key requirement is that you have to have a baseline fluency in SAP terminology. A comfortable ease with SAP and industry terms signals to your coworkers and clients that you know what you're doing. Talking the talk is critical, but if you can't walk the walk, it will eventually catch up with you.)

Your Job Plan

Having a plan for your job search will increase your chances of success. As the saying goes, hope is not a plan. Firing off your resume to random job postings you come across is not a plan. In order to compete in the marketplace for high-paying SAP jobs, you need to come up with a plan of attack. To do so you first need to understand the *people* who can offer you a job. Regardless of what role you are after, it is a *person* who can offer you a job, not a company. You need to try to put yourself in the shoes of a hiring manager and figure out how to rise above the clutter of candidates vying for their attention. And make no mistake, for every open SAP position there are hundreds of candidates and recruiters angling to get in the door and land the job.

Let me give you some insight about how the process works in the real world with customers that are hiring for a business analyst or developer role, with an example from my job as Director of SAP Applications at an SAP customer. When I need to hire a new SAP team member, I first get in touch with our internal HR person. I tell him that I'm looking to hire for a position and supply him with a job description. The job description will be something written earlier that I am reusing, perhaps changing it slightly for different functional areas. I don't have time to do frequent updates to job descriptions. Every so often I may do a refresh or rewrite of the job description, but typically I just send something over to HR that I have in my files. I mention this because I frankly don't remember if I require five years of experience or seven, or whether the candidate *must* have global deployment experience or if it's just a nice thing to have. You should never take yourself out of the running for a job just because you don't match the written job requirements exactly. I may not remember the exact requirements myself! What I'm looking for is a good employee, and if you can convince me you are that person then I really don't care what the job description specifies; after all, I wrote it, so I can certainly change my mind. On the other hand, I do know that I require some years of SAP experience, so you're wasting your time applying if your qualifications are completely off the mark for a given position. If you are in the ballpark in terms of the job requirements, don't be your own worst critic and not even try for a position just because you are a couple years off the "required" experience level. Once I send that job requisition and description to the HR guy (let's call him Gary), he will post it on the company website. He may then post it on a jobs website. Our guy uses Monster.com because the company posts all of our jobs there, even the SAP ones. Frankly, I've never found Monster to be useful for SAP jobs personally, but it seems to be some HR policy to use it. Additionally, he may make a post on an SAP-specific job site per my request such as AllSAPJobs.com. He may also put a job posting on LinkedIn, which is becoming more and more relevant for job searches these days. If he's not getting a good response or the quality of applicants is low, he may then reach out to a small set of recruiters to help him in the search. He won't have to reach out very far because we are deluged with recruiting companies trying to place people, both contract and permanent. Resumes will be submitted to him from these sources. Depending on the type of position, how it was advertised, how long it stays open, etc., he is going to receive anywhere from 5–500 resumes for an SAP position, as well as many inquiries from recruiting firms and body shops. As he receives the resumes, he does a quick quality check on them: Does it look like this person has SAP experience? If the requirement is for an SD analyst, does it say she worked in SD anywhere on the resume? This is the first step in winnowing down the volume and providing quality control and is one way he adds value for me, the hiring manager. He filters out candidates who are obviously not qualified for the position so that I don't have to review hundreds of resumes. Other companies use HR software to accomplish the same goal of separating the wheat from the chaff. Resumes that pass this step will be sent on to me for a quick review. I'm usually busy with many other activities on any given day, so I will open each resume and spend around two minutes perusing it before I make a decision as to whether to go further with that candidate. For example, Gary might send me an email with five resumes attached. I'll then reply back to him, "Gary, follow up on Abe, Sajal, and Michele and drop the others." Sometimes he'll send me one resume at a time. He will often include a *candidate summary* in addition to the resume. This is a big value add for me because it succinctly summarizes many of the points I'll be looking for in the resume and in the candidate. In our case, we look at years of SAP experience, years of specific industry experience, communication skills, personality and "cultural fit." Having a candidate summary saves me time in going through each resume and gives me a quick snapshot of the candidates.

After I choose the resumes I want to follow up on, the next step for Gary is to hold a screening call with the candidates. This is another area where HR adds value for me. They save me time by pre-qualifying the candidates and filtering out candidates who don't meet some basic criteria. Here are his screening criteria:

- Basic communication skills: Can he understand the candidate? You might be surprised at how many applicants are unintelligible on the phone. To be brutally honest, we are an American business, and the language of American business is American English. If our people can't understand a word you're saying, it really doesn't matter how great your technical skills are; you won't be of much use to us if no one can understand you. Many SAP candidates come from countries outside the US, with India being the most common source. If your accent is so heavy to the American ear that Gary can't understand anything you're saying, you are not going to make the cut. Here's a tip: *slow it down and cut the technical jargon!* Always keep your audience in mind. You're talking to someone in HR who knows very little about SAP, so don't start spewing about BADIs, ABAP, and webdynpros in rapid fire. You might have lots of great things to say on these topics, but this is not the time—this is not a technical interview. Think about all the time you spent learning SAP, then spend a little time honing your communication skills.

  Note: do not use a mobile phone unless you have an excellent connection, because it makes it that much more difficult to communicate clearly.
- Do you have close to the required number of years of SAP experience?
- Do you have some specific module experience, if required?
- Are your salary expectations in line with what we are paying? If not, Gary will tell you, but if you insist on $150K and we are targeting $120K max, you won't move forward. If you're really interested in the company, this isn't the time to play

hardball with numbers. Wait until you've got us hooked and we really want you!

- If we have any restrictions with Visa sponsorship, we'll need to understand your situation.

The most common failures in this initial HR screening process are:

1. Gary could barely understand the candidate. He sort of understood them until they got excited two minutes into it and started talking super-fast about something technical—then he just gave them the courtesy "uh-huh" during pauses for breath. She thought he understood her, but he didn't.
2. The candidate wanted too much money.

If you pass these basic screening criteria, he will ask me if I want to do a phone interview or an in-person interview with you. I will usually say yes to a thirty-minute call or an hour-long in-person interview if the candidate is local or if we have a timing constraint (i.e., the candidate has another offer, seems especially appealing, etc.).

After the call, assuming I'm still interested, I'll do an in-person interview, or a Skype interview if travel isn't possible. As part of the interview I will usually do a "technical interview," during which I attempt to ascertain whether the candidate knows their SAP. I may bring in a current team member if it's an area I am not particularly knowledgeable in, such as finance. If we're still interested, I'll have the candidate meet my boss, other appropriate members of my team, or relevant businesspeople.

Remember that the HR person's job to act as a gatekeeper for me. Nobody has the time or the desire to sort through hundreds of resumes. Your job is to keep from getting filtered out and to make it to the second step: the interview with the hiring manager. Again, the filters are:

1. Resume: Do you have "enough" SAP experience? Can I understand or relate to your experience? Does your resume look suspicious?
2. HR phone interview: Can Gary understand you? Can you articulate your experience? Can you articulate why you are interested in the position? Are your salary expectations in line with what the position offers?
3. Hiring manager interview. Can you articulate your experience? Can you articulate why you are interested in the position? Do you seem motivated and interested in the position? Why did you leave your last position? Are you going to fit in with the team and culture? Are you emotionally stable? Am I going to be able to justify hiring you? Do I like you? Do you have the technical skills necessary for the role? Do you have the people skills necessary for the role?

Think of the above as the standard process and the list of hurdles you have to overcome to make it to the goal line. Alternate routes also exist that have different challenges but are more effective and increase your odds of getting hired. One of these is getting in front of me (the hiring manager) *directly*. For example, if you are somebody I already know and think well of, your chances of being hired go up exponentially. If you are relatively new to the SAP field, the chances of that happening are small. However, second best is if you are referred to me by someone in my network. For example, I might get an email like this:

Hi John,

I understand you are looking for an SAP resource. I'm forwarding you the resume of Joe Blaze, whom I know from company Y. He's pretty junior but is really eager and a fast learner. Hope all is well.

Phil

The chances of you knowing someone directly in my network are not all that high but are definitely higher than your chances of knowing me directly. These days, with the popularity of professional social networks such as LinkedIn, this type of network referral is much easier to get than it was in the past. The founder of LinkedIn, Reid Hoffman, says that three degrees of separation is the maximum effective range for recommendations, meaning that for a recommendation to have impact, the person you are trying to access must actually know the person you are asking for an introduction. So if you have a contact named Raj, he can put you in contact with Bob. Bob may know Phil, who knows me (the hiring manager). You cannot go directly to me or Phil or Bob, because none of us knows you. Your best option in this case is to ask Raj to introduce you to Bob as an eager new SAP person looking for advice on getting a position. At the very least, Bob (or Raj) may be able to give you some advice. At best, he may later introduce you to Phil. Sorting out these connections may seem challenging, but it's actually very easy on LinkedIn. Be sure to set up a LinkedIn profile that highlights any SAP experience you have and your interest in the SAP world. You should also join LinkedIn SAP groups, such as ASUG, your regional

ASUG (you should go to the regional meetings, too), SAP Community, SAP Jobs, and others. Just search "SAP" on LinkedIn to get a full list.

A second strategy which we'll call the indirect approach is to avoid the HR screening funnel altogether. It works like this:

1. You search for open SAP positions on AllSAPJobs.com. This site is an SAP jobs aggregator, meaning it pulls in SAP jobs from other companies' websites, usually customers. This is a good site if you are targeting a business analyst or end user role. There are also other non-SAP job aggregators such as Simply Hired and Indeed.

2. Once you find a position that interests you, search the company name along with the keyword "SAP" on LinkedIn. Chances are you'll be able to find either a hiring manager or someone in the hiring manager's network. You can also try searching with "IT" or "CIO," which may help you find the right person. Finding the right person is the goal here.

3. Once you've found the right person, search for them on LinkedIn. You want to get a message to that person about what a fantastic candidate you are. Here's an example:

Dear Mr. Jones,

My name is Jerry Smith. I am an aspiring X (Business Analyst/ABAPer/etc.). I've been working/studying/training in SAP X (SD/MM/programming) over the past six months, and I'm looking for a company where I can apply my energy, enthusiasm, and learning to help solve the company's challenges. I'm willing to do whatever it takes to get my foot in the door and prove my value, including coming in as an intern and working for free. I'm sure you get many candidates and recruiters knocking on your door, many of whom have more experience on their resumes than I do. I think I can supply some things that many of them can't, and if I could just have a quick five-minute phone conversation with you I hope to convince you of the same.

Thanks so much for your consideration!

Jerry (jerry@yahoo.com)
(949) 455-8392

This kind of personalized, heartfelt message can go a long way toward breaking through the clutter. There is not a day that goes by that I don't get a LinkedIn invitation from someone *I don't even know,* with just the standard linked verbiage about "I'd like to connect." I rarely accept a request to connect with a total stranger, especially one who has not taken the time to personalize a message and tell me why I might want to connect with them. These people come across as trolling for connections and are "networkers" in the pejorative sense of the word.

Another alternative avenue into a company is finding a connection to anyone who works at the target company and asking them to pass your resume on to the hiring manager. Even if I as the hiring manager don't know this co-worker, I nonetheless feel like I need to pay a bit more attention to the resume because the co-worker may follow up with me. It's in the interest of good relations with my work colleagues for me to pay attention to referred candidates. The candidate has their credibility boosted by the fact that someone already working at the company is willing to vouch for them. Another option is getting to my boss—if my boss refers you to me, that's an especially influential referral.

When I have a position open, I may reach out to my own network of SAP contacts to see if they are available or if they have anyone to recommend. My boss or someone on my team may also refer a candidate. With a direct referral, you may be able to skip the first couple of steps and avoid getting screened out on the basis of a mismatched resume or HR screening. *The more steps you can skip, the better your chances, and coming in through a referral gives you a leg up on the competition.* If the referral comes from someone inside the company or a close colleague of myself or my boss then you have a big head start. This is why it's critical to build and maintain your SAP network as you grow your career. It's an old SAP truism that it's a small world in SAP and that there are probably only one to three degrees of separation between SAP workers due to the nature of project work. If you do good or bad work on a project, there is probably someone on the next one who will find out about it, which could make or break your next opportunity.

Recruiters

If my HR guy Gary isn't able to find quality candidates through the company website or by other means, his next step is to reach out to a recruiting company. Usually this just means he picks up his phone for a change, because recruiters are constantly calling trying to connect with him or me. It's gotten so bad that I don't pick up my desk phone anymore because it's invariably someone trying to sell me something. Recruiters are people or companies that act as middlemen between a client's staffing needs and the candidates who can fill them. Rather than having to screen through hundreds of candidates, we can just hand our requirements off to a recruiter and in the next few days get a nice, short list of candidates who are qualified and ready to work. Recruiters scout candidates for both "perm" positions, which are permanent and full-time, and contract positions, which involve hourly projects. Some companies specialize in one or the other, but most do both. The recruiting world is wild and wooly and there are varying degrees of competence, knowledge, and honesty among recruiters. In my experience, the least effective ones are those that try to do it all rather than specializing in SAP. These general IT contracting companies try to cover every technology: Microsoft, Oracle, database administration, network engineering, and so on. Then it's "Oh, yes, we do SAP too." The problem with this approach is that SAP is a very specific and deep field, and to add any value you have to understand at least the basics of the different roles, what they do, the modules, and the technologies. Bad recruiters inundate us with resumes that are off the mark and waste our time. The good ones are easy to work with and responsive, and they know what they're doing. All we have to do is tell them what we're looking for and they go to work posting ads and searching their networks for qualified candidates. Next, they review resumes and screen the candidates before presenting us with a nice package of applicants that usually includes the resume in the recruiter's format, a brief summary of the candidate, and an explanation of why they would be a good fit for our company. The more information we give the recruiter, the more effective they can be, but the good ones also use their knowledge of the company, its culture, and other factors to find the right person for the job.

Here's an example of a recent recruiter's summary I received:

Sandeep Gupta

- Located in Atlanta
- Green Card holder
- Working with in apparel industry now on X project
- Been with current consulting company (Y for 8 ½ years)
- Motivation: Had been wanting to find a full-time career with an end client once his green card was received, which is now the case
- SAP 10 years
- SD/EDI focus
- MM, WM integration
- 4 full lifecycle projects
- $115k base salary target + relocation funds

This gives me a ten-second snapshot of the candidate so I don't have to wade through a long resume. I can immediately tell from this short list how much experience the candidate has, his visa status, why he's looking to move, and how much money he wants. This is the information I need to decide whether I want to invest my time in going further with the candidate or not. In my busy world, this is invaluable, because I don't have a lot of time to read through a mountain of resumes.

So why am I boring you with the inner world of a hiring manager? Because this type of summary is *exactly* what you should be using to market yourself. You should absolutely have a summary section at the top of your resume, and you should include it in email communications and as talking points when discussing your background during phone screens. The easier you make it on the people searching for candidates, the better your chances of landing the job.

Types of Job Targets

As was discussed earlier, there are different roles (Functional/Technical) and different types of companies (Customers/Consulting Firms). Depending on what kind of company and role you're targeting, you may want to tweak your approach a little.

Customers

At a general level, the roles within a customer (companies that have implemented or are implementing SAP) are:

Business Analyst: This is a Functional SAP role within a company. These are the people who will inherit or have already inherited the ongoing support of the company's SAP system from the project team. Depending on the company, they may do strictly production support (bug fixes, issue resolution, extending functionality) or they may handle new deployments of functionality, new business units, new geographical deployments, etc.

Developer: This is a technical SAP role within a company. The developer is involved in all of the above activities on the ABAP programming side of things. Developers typically focus on RICEF (Reports, Interfaces, Conversions, Enhancements, and Forms) items.

Basis: This is the in-house basis administrator who handles SAP system administration.

Security: This involves in-house security administration of user roles and authorizations.

Consulting Companies
Within a consulting company one can find a wide range of SAP project roles including:

Functional Consultant, Technical Consultant, Basis, Security, Change Management, Training, Project Management, Auditing, and more.

First Steps

If you are new to SAP then you have the challenge of how to get some SAP experience under your belt without having the SAP experience employers look for when hiring. This catch-22 isn't unique to SAP, and you're not the first person who's had to overcome this obstacle. It can be done. I was lucky enough to be hired by SAP America in 1997 during a time when demand for consultants was outpacing supply. As a result, during the mid-90s SAP America responded by ramping up hiring of recent MBA graduates and putting them through boot camps where we drank SAP through a fire hose. At that time, SAP's approach in the US was to hire people who had some degree of business experience, or a business degree, and then train them up in an SAP functional module. I can still remember my frustration at trying to understand even the most basic sales order concepts in SD. Nothing we learned seemed intuitive and very little of it made sense to me as I was going through training. It was only after being thrown into my first project that things began to sink in and make sense.

Unless you get lucky, your chances of getting hired and put through SAP training at SAP America or a consulting company aren't very good these days. The market is too mature and there are too many folks out there with real or imaginary experience on their resumes for companies to invest in lengthy training for newly hired consultants.

Here are some suggestions for gaining that first critical SAP experience.

Option 1 - Get a job at a customer

If you work for a company that runs SAP, chances are pretty good that you can find a role in which you can become an end user of the software. At a minimum, you can establish a relationship with someone who is an SAP user and ask to take five minutes each day to watch them do their job. Make sure your boss and others around the workplace know that you are keen to learn SAP, and ask if there is any work you can do on your own time to help out. Send the CIO or SAP Director a note letting them know that you are enthusiastic and would love to learn SAP skills, and ask what they recommend. The point is that once you are on the inside, you have a lot more options that would be closed to you otherwise. See the appendix for a list of potential target companies.

Option 2 - Take an unpaid internship at an SAP consulting company or a company running SAP

Again, make clear your desire and enthusiasm to learn and help. These days, internship opportunities are often posted on job sites such as Dice.com or AllSAPJobs.com.

Option 3 - Training

These days there are plenty of options when it comes to self-training. A Google search for SAP training will return a multitude of results. The online training world is a little dicey, so use caution. Don't spend a lot of money on an online training course. Technical folks who know another programming language might want to buy a book on ABAP and then find a company that offers training system access. Those interested in functional roles should pick a module to focus on and buy a book or other materials. *Do not* spend tens of thousands of dollars on a "Certification Course." When I was at SAP, the idea of offering a certification program came up every year and was rejected. Who would certify? What would the consulting partners say? Who would care about a certification? Who would be dumb enough to pay extra for it? Well, it looks like we were wrong; SAP eventually offered a "certification" program (as a revenue generator for the training department is my guess), and lo and behold a lot of folks (mostly newbies) went for it and it gained traction. But let me tell you this: as a hiring manager, I really couldn't care less when someone says they are a "certified" SD consultant. I want to know that they have work experience and are knowledgeable in a given SAP area. A certification doesn't tell me that. Frankly, I don't know what goes into being "certified," and I've seen all kinds of cheat sheets and more on the internet. A certification doesn't impress me. If you want to spend your money, spend it on improving your communication skills, career coaching, SAP books, or access to an SAP training system that will let you practice your skills. Companies that charge tens of thousands of dollars for this stuff are ripping you off, and they're not getting you much closer to a job. Having a certification is not required and isn't a differentiator.

Ten-Step Job Plan

Below is a ten-step job plan to assist you on your journey. You should always remember that **hiring is not "fair."** You are not in school and hiring is not an objective meritocracy. The best candidate doesn't always get the job. The candidate who gets the job is the one who is the most convincing and likable, and, most importantly, the one who gets in front of the right people at the right time. In the end, a hiring manager needs to "buy" you as a candidate. You are selling yourself, and studies have shown that purchasing decisions are more often based on emotion than logic. People use logic to justify the emotional decision they have already made, so get in front of them, be confident, and be likable!

Here's the plan:

1. Resume
2. LinkedIn Profile
3. Training/Self-Study
4. Internship
5. Networking/Interviewing
6. End User or Production Support
7. Super User
8. Business Analyst or Developer
9. Consultant
10. Independent Contractor

1. Resume

Your resume is your starting point and the place you'll return to again and again during your SAP career journey. This is your face to the world of potential employers. It says who you are professionally and why you are worth bothering about. It should help employers think about how you can help solve their problems. There are plenty of books and online resources about resume writing. There is a good deal of subjectivity regarding this topic, but for an SAP resume in particular, this is what I find effective.

- A name that I can envision pronouncing. You don't have to change your name to Bob Smith, but if your name is Rajakranthantpanja Veludalna Krishnavarassanatva, you may want to put just "Raj Krishna" at the top of your resume. This isn't a legal document, and if I have to worry about how I'm going to say your name when I call you up for a phone interview, it may just give a slight edge to another candidate who has a less intimidating name. Not fair, I know, but *don't do anything to make it hard on the people reviewing your resume! Make it as easy as possible for them to give you the job!*
- A clear, succinct summary of your experience with SAP, as follows:
  - X years' SAP experience (this should include *anything* SAP, such as training, internships, etc.
  - X years' specific SAP area experience (SD, ABAP, etc.)
  - X years' work experience
  - X years' industry experience, if relevant
  - Your key positive attributes: communication skills, high energy, dedication, etc.

- o Education and awards, especially if you are light on work experience or have been awarded something significant
- o Visa status—highlight this only if you are a US citizen or green card holder; otherwise, leave it off and save it for the HR screening
- Length under five pages—longer than that is a waste of paper. You can summarize old projects and jobs if you need to.
- Clean formatting - make it easy to read. Send it off to someone for a professional cleanup if you can't manage, or use a template.
- Real projects and experience – Unfortunately, a lot of fraud goes on in the SAP job market these days. The internet is awash with people offering fake resumes, fake jobs, and even fake candidates. I don't have to prove to anyone that something is fishy on your resume; I just have to think it and I am done with you. Remember: you are going to be interviewed with this resume in front of me. If you have no clue about something that is on your resume, we are done. I've had this happen with candidates many times. If you don't know anything about something on your resume, it's all over. Exaggeration is OK—lying is fatal. There is a line between selling yourself and outright falsification; don't cross it.

2. LinkedIn Profile

Set up a LinkedIn profile, and remember that this is a landing page for potential recruiters and employers. Make sure it looks professional and matches your resume if you detail your work history. This will also be your starting point for online networking, so start adding professional contacts as you make them. A contact of a contact could be instrumental in getting you that next position. Join SAP-related groups and pay attention to the posts.

3. Training/Self-Study

You need to learn SAP if you're going to work in it. To learn SAP you can download training courses, buy used SAP books, and take a reasonably priced online training course. You can also ask friends and colleagues who are more knowledgeable what they recommend.

Join the SAP Community Network via the SCN (SCN.SAP.COM) and subscribe to different SAP marketing emails such as SAP Flash. Go on to the SAP website. Study the extensive SAP help documentation at help.sap.com. If applicable, focus on an industry and learn all about that industry's specific processes and terminology.

4. Internship

Set up job alerts on websites such as Dice, AllSAPJobs, Monster, etc. that will email you new job postings using "SAP" and search keywords such as "internship" and "entry level." See the appendix for a list of recommended job sites.

Review the list of SAP Customers in the appendix. Find out which are in your city or an area where you would like to live. Search for jobs at these companies that are not necessarily SAP-centric. For example, customer service representative, accountant, or purchasing agent. All of these roles are likely to be end users of SAP. Pursue and take one of these jobs if possible. You can also search for "SAP" and the company name from your list with the goal of finding out who runs the SAP group. Once you have their name you can then send them a personalized LinkedIn mail as we talked about earlier; offer your services as an enthusiastic intern trained up on SAP and looking for a break.

For example, I see that Epson is on the list of SAP customers. I happen to know they are in my geographical area, so I search "Epson" and "SAP" on LinkedIn and get a list of two thousand people. I narrow that down using filters to show only people with "US" and "Current Company" as Epson or Epson America, which leaves me with a final list of forty-two people. Of these, I can quickly scan through or refine my search further until I see people who have some degree of SAP responsibility at their company. I see someone named Vikas R., who is a senior IT executive in the SAP area. Perfect. These are the type of people I want to reach out to with a personalized message. Every SAP person remembers when they were the new guy trying to break in, so only the most hardened will have no sympathy for folks in a similar boat.

5. Interviews

Let me let you in on a secret: I have conducted hundreds of interviews over my career and I have never received any formal training or guidance on what questions to ask or how an interview should be structured. This includes my many years at SAP America as a manager and director, as well as my time at my last company as director of SAP applications. The only guidance I've been given has concerned what questions not to ask (i.e., the discriminatory type such as whether the applicant is married or goes to church). Half the time when I am giving an interview I've had very little time to prepare. I'm typically in the middle of something urgent when the reminder pops up in Outlook that I've got an interview in fifteen minutes, and I think "Oh, crap. I better look at this person's resume first and remind myself who it is I'll be talking with." I'm telling you this because anything you can do to make me feel good during this process is going to be to your benefit. Be positive, tell a joke, be nice—anything to forge at least a tentative emotional connection with me as a human being. Another reason why this is relevant is that I don't have a set agenda of questions. This means you can steer the conversation toward your strengths and away from your weaknesses. If you don't have much SAP work experience, for God's sake don't announce that right away. Instead, do everything you can to highlight your positive qualities: you're a dedicated and hard worker, you're a quick learner. Take an interest in me, too. Don't be an obvious suck-up, but remember that most people love to talk about their favorite subject—themselves!

Even though I've had no formal instruction, I have come up with my own methods over the years. I usually start out by getting the person to describe their career by asking how they got started in SAP or what they've been up to lately. What I'm trying to get a sense of upfront is how this person communicates. Can they describe something to me in a way I'll understand? Do they pause at appropriate intervals or do they ramble on forever? Do they pick up on body language? This is a chance for you to tell a nice, succinct story about yourself. Don't go into excruciating detail. This is also your chance to lighten things up. We are probably both a little bit uncomfortable (maybe you more than me). If you can work in something humorous, I may get the feeling that you would be nice to have around. Don't complain, and don't reveal too much personal detail such as how you need the job because your ex-wife is hounding you for child support. I didn't ask.

Next, I'll ask about some particular project experience. What was your role? How did it go? I might ask you what your key strengths are. I will always ask why you are interested in the position. I will ask you some SAP questions relating to the role you are applying for. For example, I frequently ask SD folks to describe how pricing works in SD because a) they better know this since it is a fundamental SD concept called the "condition technique", and b) even more important, I like to get a sense of how well they can explain something. Do they explain it in a coherent manner, or do they jump all around from pricing procedure directly to condition tables? Do they explain the topic in a structured manner that makes sense? Do they try to gauge their audience's reaction and understanding of their description? Can I picture the candidate working with a business user and explaining the topic coherently? I will always ask if they have questions for me. They better! And it should be more than one. If not, they will strike me as not too interested or not bright enough to be concerned about what kind of place they might end up working at.

Red Flags - things **never** to do in an interview (these are all taken from actual interviews that I've given over the years.)
- Don't lie - if you don't know, say what you know, and leave it at that. I respect people much more who are direct about something they don't know or don't have experience with something than those who try to fake it.

- Don't try to cover up fake items on your resume. If your resume says you were a team lead but you were only doing production support don't dig yourself in to a deeper hole when I start to ask about your duties on that project. You'll look better if you correct your duties in the interview rather than trying to lie your way out of it. You'd have looked even better if you didn't lie on the resume.

- Don't refuse to answer a question. I don't care if you didn't think this was going to be a "technical interview".

- Don't bullshit me. I've been doing this awhile. I can smell BS.

- Don't talk about family problems. I'm sorry that you're divorced and have complex child custody arrangements but don't muck up the interview bring this stuff up.

- Don't talk about workplace violence. Wow, that's a great story about how co-worker came back to your last place of employment and shot people. Next!

- Don't complain about the interview. Did you expect the interview to be fun? Do you like going to the dentist too?

- Don't tell me the recruiter made you lie. This makes you sound un-ethical and weak.

- Don't ramble on forever. This is an interview, not a monologue.

- Don't badmouth other companies or people. You may be entirely justified in your comments but there's no need to introduce this kind of negativity in an interview.

- Don't talk so fast that I can't understand you. What is he saying?

- Don't talk about Visa problems. Wait till you have convinced me you are the right candidate. Then we can talk about visa issues.

- Don't do an interview with a bad phone connection. Use a landline or go somewhere where you have a good cell connection.
- Don't have someone else do your phone interview for you. I'll figure out it wasn't you when we meet in person and that will be that.
- Don't look up answers while doing a phone interview. It's dishonest and I can hear the click, click, click after each question I ask.

Things to Do

- Do have a comprehensive summary of yourself and your work experience prepared.
- Do ask questions about the company and project.
- Do pay attention to the interviewer's reactions; if he's yawning, move on.
- Do be prepared to highlight your strengths.
- Do be prepared to discuss a weakness of your choice. This is a classic. Yes, I know—you work too hard!
- Do be prepared for a technical interview.
- Do be patient and flexible. Your interview may be rescheduled at the last minute, and you may not hear back from the company as soon as you would like. Take it in stride.
- Do project a positive and energetic demeanor.
- Do say you can travel if needed (unless you absolutely can't).
- Do let the interviewer know (if you can slip it in) that you are speaking with several different companies. Just as in dating, this makes you seem more desirable and increases the sense of urgency for the company to pursue you.
- Do the interview in person if you are given the option. This brings you one step closer to getting hired if you make a good impression.
- Do tailor your communication to the person who is interviewing you. Don't talk table structures with business executives, but do talk about them with SAP folks if appropriate.

6. End User/Production Support

Assuming you've been able to garner some kind of SAP experience on your resume, whether from an internship or online training, your next goal is to land a paying job. The most direct route for many is to join a company running SAP as a member of a production support team. Production support teams take care of live SAP systems, whether in-house as employees of the company using SAP or as part of a services company that provides outsourced production support to companies on a contractual basis. When pursuing that first paying job, you are going to have to emphasize your strengths (energy, enthusiasm, drive, communication skills, customer focus) and downplay your weakness (not much actual SAP work experience).

An alternative path into a paying SAP gig is landing a job as an end user at a company that uses SAP. Depending on your background, you could be an accountant, a customer service agent, or a programmer for a legacy application. Once you get hired at a company, you are in a good position to become an end user or to express interest in being an end user; you'll have a much better chance of moving into an end user role than if you were coming from the outside. Once you are an end user, two things happen:

1. Your SAP experience clock starts ticking. For example, you may be an accountant just entering journal entries into SAP, but your resume can now legitimately say "SAP FICO Experience." Being a user is your gateway into learning the functionality and then the configuration behind it.
2. You gain entry into a network of more experienced SAP people if you choose to pursue it. From the departmental super user to the production support team to consultants

implementing a project, you now have the ability to make connections, learn from those more experienced than you, and grow your network.

Working with Recruiters

Anyone working in the SAP world for a while is going to have some interaction with recruiters. Recruiters are the middlemen between SAP workers and SAP employers. They assist companies in finding the right people (and sometimes the wrong people) to fill open positions, both permanent and contract. Recruiters run the gamut in terms of ability, knowledge, and professionalism. Some know their SAP very well, and are honest and professional, and some...not so much.

Recruiters typically work with a company to try to understand what the company is looking for in a candidate. They then search for candidates, screen out those who don't match the requirements, present the client with a summary and resume for each candidate, and facilitate negotiations. For perm placements, the recruiting company is usually paid a portion of the first-year salary of the hire, typically around 30 percent. Companies are usually inundated with recruiters offering their services, so they tend to use a limited number of them with whom they've established a relationship.

For contract consulting roles, the process works a bit differently. Typically, an implementation project will have a primary consulting partner the client has hired to manage the implementation. This partner is known as the "prime" in industry parlance. The prime tries to fill any consulting roles needed with their own employees first, because they make more money on their own salaried people and because they have more leverage over an employee. If they are not able to fill a spot with one of their own employees, they look at external resources. For the large consulting companies that are usually the prime contractor (Accenture, Deloitte, Cap Gemini, IBM, and these days often Indian companies such as Tata, Wipro, L&T, etc.) it doesn't make sense for them to have agreements with thousands of independent contractors. They send their requisition for a resource out to a number of their certified vendors, who then reach out to the market to find somebody to fill the need.

Some of the better companies have their own databases of consultants they've worked with in the past whom they will reach out to. However, more often than not, these companies just blast out ads on Dice.com and start trolling for resumes. There will often be multiple postings for the same position because each of these small companies is trying to be the first one to land a candidate that the prime will accept. When the ad garners a response from a candidate with a reasonable-looking resume, there will be a quick call to the candidate to verify an acceptable hourly rate and availability. There is usually no formal interview, and the candidate's resume is quickly sent off to the prime or client for review. The secondary companies make their money on the spread between what the prime will pay and what they can negotiate with the consultant. For example, the customer may be billed $200/hour by the prime, and the prime may pay $150/hour to the secondary vendor, who will pay the consultant $130/hour, earning the secondary $20/hour for as long as the consultant is engaged and earning the prime $50/hour.

In discussions with recruiting vendors (also known as "body shops"), it's important to remember that there is usually room for negotiation on rates. The recruiting vendor you are dealing with will rarely tell you the rate they're getting. Even if they do, you won't know whether to believe them or not. A fair amount of subterfuge goes on; some recruiters lie, cheat, and steal. Trust your instincts. If something seems shady, it probably is! Keep in mind that you have no obligation to any one recruiter until they bring you something. Don't feel bad about applying to multiple postings for the same position and playing recruiters off against each other in negotiations. Remember: you never know what they are really getting paid, and they won't take any deal that will lose them money. Recruiters usually have a two-tiered system. The first person who calls you will be the delivery person, who interfaces with and weeds out the candidates. Once you are past the delivery person, they will pass you on to the sales person, who has a relationship with the prime or customer. These people usually know more about the project details than the screeners, though sometimes neither knows much. After your call with the sales person, your next interview will probably be with the prime or the end client to see what they think of you. If you convince them, you're in!

7. Consultant

"Yes, I look forward to traveling 100 percent of the time. I can even do 110 percent!" Big consulting companies look for candidates with maximum flexibility in terms of being able to travel to client sites for projects (Note - the interview is not the time to negotiate for a local project!) Consulting companies are good places to be for a readymade network of colleagues and access to training. The major benefit over independent contracting is that you don't have to find your own projects. That's what the partners at the consulting firms do for you during their golf games with the customer's executives. The salaries in consulting are high relative to other industries, but not as high as independent contracting. There is a variety among the various consulting firms, and one of the things to consider is the career paths available if you plan on staying for a long time. Consulting companies are great places to get exposure to different companies, industries, and people as you travel the country and work on different client projects.

8. Independent Contracting

Independent contracting is an attractive option for many SAP folks because there is the potential to earn very good money. This is the pot of gold at the end of the proverbial rainbow for SAP folks. Of all the various SAP job roles—business analyst, consultant, etc.—independent contractors typically have the highest potential upside in terms of compensation.

This makes sense if you think about how consulting companies operate. In a nutshell, a Big 4 (or any other) consulting company typically bills out its consultants to a client company at an hourly rate, let's say $250/hour, for a senior SAP consultant. Then they pay their consultants a salary and a bonus. A consultant who is making $150,000 a year is getting paid roughly $78/hour with vacations and holidays. That difference of $250 - $78 = $172/hour is going to the consulting company. No wonder the partners are rich! The consulting company is essentially a middleman between the client and the consultant, and wherever there is a middleman, that middleman is going to take his cut, in this case quite a substantial one. The more layers of middlemen involved between you and client, the less money will be available to go around. The ideal situation is to have a direct billing relationship with the end customer, though this is often difficult to achieve. Of course, the consulting company offers you many things: they find you that next project, they may offer training, they still pay you a salary when you are on the bench (not on a project), and they offer benefits such as health insurance and a 401k plan. Many consultants, however, especially as they become more experienced, find that they can do much better for themselves. They can easily incorporate their own company and become an independent contractor. They can find their own contract positions through job sites such as Dice, through recruiters, and through their own network. Of course, it's not all wine and roses in the contracting world. Sometimes it's not easy to find a project, there are unscrupulous recruiters and body shops, and there are other middlemen that take their cut. There is also cheap offshore labor to contend with that pushes rates down for everyone else. On the other hand, a positive aspect of independent contracting is that you have the flexibility to decide when and where you want to take project work. If you want to take a three-month vacation, take one. Of course, you won't get paid during that time, but that's up to you and not some corporate policy that says you only get three weeks a year. If you don't want to fly cross country to a client site, you don't have to and you won't get the stink eye from any boss if you say "no". You can always choose to wait for another project to come along. Of course, with freedom comes responsibility. If you don't work, you don't get paid, so you have an incentive not to be overly choosy.

Project Skills - Surviving and Thriving After You Land the Job

Once you've finally made your way onto your first SAP project, the fun begins! There are a number of pitfalls you'd be wise to avoid in order to stay on a project and make it to the finish line. Getting that first project under your belt will make it much easier to get onto the next one. Here are three tips to help you on your way:

When working on a project, always remember rule #1 -

Rule #1 - The business is the dog, IT is the tail.

The tail doesn't wag the dog! As someone once said, there is no such thing as an IT project, only business projects which may have a large IT components. Always strive to keep the business users satisfied first. If you keep the business folks happy without alienating IT too much, you will thrive. IT and consulting firms will have a very hard time getting rid of a consultant whom the business loves. The converse is not true. Always go the extra mile to help the business people. They are your key to your project longevity.

Rule #2 - You don't need to know everything, you just need to know more than the person you are supporting.

Being new, you are going to be nervous. What if you don't know the answer to a question? Will you appear inexperienced and incompetent? Here's a handy consulting trick to prevent these embarrassing situations.

- If asked something you don't know the answer to, look distracted and say you are in the middle of something but that you'd love to dig into that topic. Schedule a meeting time, and prepare like hell.

- Try to address topics in a deliberate and planned manner so that you can prepare ahead of time for the particular topic. Try to keep the discussion focused on the topic that was planned.
- Prepare like hell. This means nights back at the hotel, weekends, airplane rides, etc. should be used to prepare for any tasks, meetings, or presentations you have coming up.

It's like the old joke about two guys out in the woods who start talking.

One guy says, "If a bear came after us, I'd get away."

The other says, "There's no way. Bears can outrun even the fastest person alive!"

The first guy says, "I don't have to outrun the bear, I just have to outrun you."

The analog is that you just have to stay one step ahead of the client. You can achieve this through preparation and homework. Eventually, you will internalize all of this SAP stuff, but until then, be like the boys scouts and always be prepared!

Rule #3 - Soft Skills are *very* important

Soft skills are as important as, if not more important than, technical skills. Yet technical people tend to underrate them. That's not surprising given that technical people are by definition 'technical'. Folks who work with software are attracted to logic, systems and rules. The realm of the touchy feely can make us a little uncomfortable. But it is within the realm of the soft stuff that one can find the keys to project success. Building relationships with people can make the difference between success and failure on a project. Clients and co-workers who like you are willing to offer up support, help, and co-operation. Those who don't build up relationships are apt to be ignored and given the cold shoulder. Be a pleasant person to work with! Say hello to the receptionist when you come in to work and always be nice to administrative assistants. You will stand out among a group of heads-down technologists if you are sociable and pleasant to have around.

But there is more to having good soft skills than just being friendly and pleasant. In your work habits be organized and proactive. Take the initiative, and tackle tough topics that others avoid. Communicate clearly both verbally and in writing. Schedule meetings well in advance and publish an agenda prior to the meeting. Show up on time and keep meetings on-topic. Publish meeting notes and action items post-meeting. Then follow up on the action items. Simple things like this will impress your clients and coworkers and distinguish you from the herd, as well as help keep you and your team effective and efficient.

Independent Contracting

Perhaps you've been working as a developer, business analyst or consultant for a few years and have built up a decent level of expertise in SAP. Or perhaps you've recently completed your visa sponsorship process and now have a green card. You've heard about the good money to be made for independent contractors and you're considering the options. You may be hesitant about taking the plunge into the unknown. After all, if you work for a consulting firm you probably make decent money, more than average and most likely more than you would if you were working directly for the customer. You probably get more vacation time too, and you're covered for health insurance. On the other hand, you have to get on a plane every week and your weekends consist of catching up on sleep, doing bills, taking care of the laundry and fighting with your spouse about who has it tougher. You have to travel to whatever client your jerk of a boss sends you to, and to top it off, the company you work for has been scaling back your bonus package and raising the contribution amounts for insurance. They are even laying people off if they sit on the bench too long. So much for job security!

If you have an inkling that independent contracting might be for you, the first thing I recommend is that you *do the math*. The contracting world is all about hourly rates, so what you need to do is break down your current salary and benefits into an hourly rate so you can quickly compare apples to apples. Let's say you're an SAP business analyst who makes $110,000 a year and usually gets a $10K bonus. You get health insurance and a 401k contribution. Go online and price out health insurance for you and your family so you'll know what you would pay on the open market. It's not cheap! Then subtract what you have to contribute for health insurance at work. Add all this up. Let's say it comes out to $129,000 a year. (Note: I would be hesitant to rely on HR-supplied total benefits information from your company, as the ones I have seen strike me as inflated.)

$110,000 Base salary
$ 10,000 Annual bonus
$ 5,000   401k company contribution
$ 6,000   Price of health insurance on the open market
$ - 2,000 Amount you contribute for health insurance at your company

$129,000 Total compensation

Divide that $129,000 by 52 work weeks a year at 40 hours a week to arrive at your current hourly wage, in this case $62/hr. You should keep this number in the back of your mind as you evaluate contracting opportunities. How much more than the $x/hr you currently make do you need to compensate for the risk of going into business for yourself? What happens between contracts—would you be making enough to get by in those times? Let's say the business analyst in our example is offered a contract for $110/hr. That's almost double what she is making per hour! This means she could go six months without work and make the same money she is making now. That's a lot of time to look for the next project—and take some vacation time to boot.

Another important thing to realize is that you don't need to quit your current job in order to look for contracting work; in fact, it's much better to look while you are working. Having the safety net of a stable income means you don't have to panic and accept a contract that is less than ideal. You also won't feel rushed and can compare what you have to what could be next.

Once you have decided to take the plunge into the independent contracting world, it's time to think about search strategies. I recommend setting up multiple job search agents on Dice.com. One can be for your ideal contract, perhaps targeting a specific location or role. For me, for example, the ideal contract is something local and high-paying, so I set up a search agent with the search term "SAP SD" and a local geography. Unfortunately, rate is not something that can be reliably searched for (the most common rate listing is "market," which is a useless indicator), so I can't include it as a search criterion. The rate discussion comes later. I make sure to have the search results emailed to me *daily* because speed of response is absolutely critical. Another way to search is to focus on a narrow skill set if you are more open to travel or relocation; narrower search terms will reflect a wider geographic area. But wait, we are not quite done. I set up a second search agent for a wider geography at the state level, also with "SAP SD" as a search term, because there may be an opportunity that is less than ideal but not too far away that I would like to know about. Maybe it's just outside the zip code or area codes I used to indicate my geographical preferences. I might set the results of this search to be emailed to me weekly. But wait, there's still more! I also set up a search agent with the search term "SAP" and a local geography with a weekly email. Why? Won't that deluge me in all sorts of non-relevant information? I do this because 1) I want to know about all the companies that are implementing SAP in my area; this can always come in handy when networking or talking with recruiters, 2) sometimes postings are not accurate (sometimes the recruiters don't know very much about SAP), 3) sometimes there is a niche skill I have that won't be picked up with an "SD" search, such as "pricing lead" or "ATP expert" and 4) sometimes the posting is very specific or has misspellings and you will miss it with any search term besides "SAP".

Setting up search agents on Dice is not the only way to find new contracts. Make it a habit to regularly check an SAP job aggregation website like AllSapJobs.com (fair warning: I own this site). Sites like these leverage job aggregation tools (such as Indeed) that crawl the web and scrape job postings from other websites, including company-specific job pages. This can be very handy for getting a sense of your local market in terms of hiring activity and types of roles, as well as a great place to find in-house business analyst and programming jobs as well as contract jobs not posted on Dice. All you need to do is enter your city and state and the site will return all SAP jobs from three different job aggregation tools, typically with three different sets of results. Dice has a better selection of contracting jobs, but the aggregators do better with permanent positions because HR departments always post them on their company websites; when and where they will advertise them on sites like Monster.com and Careerbuilder.com is a crapshoot.

Let's suppose you've set up your search agents. They crank along for a few weeks, and then *boom*: you see a posting that sounds good. What do you do? You reply as fast as possible via email with your resume and contact info. You don't wait until tomorrow, you don't wait until you make that final revision to your resume, you do it now! Why? Because chances are good that the recruiting company is going to send the first qualified candidate(s) they find on to the client. The client may be working with several recruiting firms, and even if they're not, if that first company doesn't find them someone quickly, they may find another company to fill the position. So, for the recruiter, and by extension for you, speed is important.

To support this process you need to have your resume (ideally several versions of it) ready to go and accessible at all times (save them on Google drive so you will have access to them anywhere). If you have time, you can highlight your most relevant experience in bold and feature it in the summary statement to tailor your resume to a particular job posting—anything to make it pop out to someone quickly scanning it. The reality is that most people spend about two minutes (if that) scanning a resume, so you should do everything you can to make your relevant experience and expertise obvious! If you don't have time for this, it's better just to get your resume submitted as quickly as possible. Once you've sent in your resume, wait an hour, and if you are excited about the position call the recruiting contact (if their phone number is listed on the posting). Typically, if a recruiter thinks you are a good fit for the position, they will call you up almost immediately after receiving your resume. Sometimes, however, they might not see your email or they have screened you out. Calling the recruiter focuses their attention on you, and you can highlight aspects of your experience they might have missed. I had just this sort of thing happen on my last contract. I sent my resume in the evening, and when I didn't hear back by mid-morning the next day I called the recruiter. It turned out that he had confused me with someone with a similar name. Then he couldn't find my resume, so I resent it while on the phone with him. He realized immediately that I was a good fit for the project and I ended up getting the position. If I hadn't called, I wouldn't have gotten the spot. A call also gives you a chance to sell yourself back into the game if you have been screened out. Perhaps the recruiter missed the relevant experience on your resume, or perhaps your clear communication skills and poise will change his mind and put you back in the game.

Rates

Contracting rates are often shrouded in secrecy. The most common rate you will see on an SAP contract job posting is "market" or "TBD." This is because keeping rates opaque benefits staffing and consulting firms. For one thing, they don't want to give the client the details of what they are actually paying the contractor for fear that the client will figure out their margin and demand a lower price. For another, they don't want to give their competition or the contractor more information than is necessary.

So what is this mysterious "market" rate? The truth is that there really isn't one. The market rate is whatever people are willing to pay and work for at a given time.

Contractor rates vary based on the experience and (perceived) expertise of the contractor, as well as on the specific SAP area, though to a smaller degree. Hot areas such as HANA tend to command somewhat higher rates, whereas skills in well-established product areas tend to pay less. As with anything, the higher the ratio of demand to supply, the higher the price; higher prices attract competition and increased supply, which brings prices down in turn.

As of this writing (2014), here is what I'm seeing in the US market in terms of market rates per hour:

Jr. Functional $80-$120
Sr. Functional $110-$160
Jr. Technical $70-$100
Sr. Technical $90-$150

A Jr. Contract resource generally has between 2-6 years SAP experience.
A Sr. Contract resource generally has 6-15+ years SAP experience.

Contracting through Consulting Companies

Consulting companies often need to augment their staff for a particular project by using independent contractors. In this sub-contracting arrangement, the consulting company takes a big slice of the hourly rate the client is paying. For example, several years back I had this arrangement:

Client X pays $225/hour to Consulting Co. Y
Consulting Co. Y pays their "Approved Vendor" $Z
"Approved Vendor" pays Contractor (me) $135/hour
Consulting Co. Y (Big 4) and "Approved Vendor" make $90/hour

This may strike you as a bit crazy. The client is paying $90/hour *extra* for the privilege of paying a consulting company (and their "Approved Vendor") for someone they could hire directly. In this case the consulting company is making $90/hour for doing virtually nothing other than passing along a bill. Each month, I bill the "Approved Vendor," the vendor bills the consulting company, and the consulting company bills the client. At each step along the way, each party dips its beak into the money and takes its cut. It went on this way for a couple of years. That adds up to around $375,000 for just one person! Eventually, the client wised up and cut out the middlemen.

So why these extra layers and inefficiencies? There are two primary reasons:

1. Big companies like to limit the number of vendors they have because they achieve efficiencies when they streamline and reduce the number of their suppliers. If every independent contractor who worked on a project was a direct vendor for the client, their accounts payable department would need to set up every one of them as a vendor and deal with the resulting paperwork and monthly billing hassles. They prefer to funnel sub-contractors through one prime contractor (the large consulting company) instead and have one point of contact.

2. Having one prime consulting company makes it easier to

manage the relationship than with a large number of consultants. If the client wants a consultant switched out, they just tell the consulting company, which takes care of it. Known as the "one throat to choke" approach, this is attractive to the client because there is just one party responsible for performance, rather than multiple independents who can point the finger at the other vendors when things go wrong.

While these are valid arguments, companies can wind up paying a very hefty price for this convenience, as noted above. Many of the more savvy IT departments will establish a direct relationship when they find a contractor with whom they want to maintain a long-term relationship, saving themselves money and allowing the contractor to earn more than they might have if they had gone through a third party.

When smaller recruiting/placement/body shop firms are involved, the markup on the contractor's rate tends to be less. For example:

Client Q pays $150/hour
Contractor is paid $120/hour
Recruiting company makes $30/hour

Another factor in the rate equation is expenses. Some clients prefer local resources because they don't have to pay the 10-15% extra on top of the rate to cover travel expenses for out-of-town consultants. In some cases, then, a local consultant can command a slightly better rate than someone coming in from out of town because the cost is still less for the client when expenses are factored in.

Negotiating

If you get a call back from a recruiting company, one of the first screening questions they are likely to ask you is "What is your rate?" or "What are your rate expectations?" You can either tell them the rate you want or ask them what rate they are looking for. Many negotiation strategies will tell you that you should let them name their price before you name yours, but I've also seen negotiation advice that tells you to cut to the chase and name your price first.

If you decide to name your rate first, always make it somewhat higher than what you actually have in mind as your target, and definitely make it higher than your absolute minimum. This gives you the chance either to get a higher rate than you expected or, more likely, to negotiate down and give the recruiter the psychological satisfaction of thinking that they were able to negotiate you down. If you ask them their own rate or the "ballpark rate," chances are they are going to quote you a range such as $105-$115 rather than a fixed amount. I believe they give a range rather than a fixed number because they can reel you in with the higher number (you hear $115) but can always end up offering you something in between. In my experience, they are doing the same thing you should be doing: creating a buffer for negotiation. When they say their top rate (or "the client's top rate") is $115, the actual top rate is probably more like $120. The recruiter is never going to tell you what the client is actually paying them (and even if they did, you would never know whether they were telling the truth).

If I was quoted a rate in the $105-$115 range, I would say something like, "Normally my rate is $135, but I could do this one for $130 because I'm interested in the company, product, location, etc." Their response will be influenced by how long they've been looking for someone, how many qualified candidates they've found, and how much of a niche skill is required for the role. You too have to take into account how interested you are in the project, where it is located, how long you've been looking, what the market is like, etc. Quite often, the first person you talk to (the candidate recruiter or screener) won't know very much about the project, so you may want to wait to play hardball on the rate until after you get past the first stage of the application process and learn more about the project. I've had recruiters tell me a project is in California only to find out during a client interview that the project team will be working in Indiana! The rate is also influenced by how many layers there are between you and the client. For example, if the layers involved can be represented by Client > Wipro > Recruiting Company > You, then there are two layers and there is less money coming down to you, in addition to a very low-cost vendor.

I also suggest having a floor rate you won't go below. For an old-timer like me, anything below three digits is where I draw the line. Anything below that and a full-time position starts to look comparable, and I would feel like I'm helping to bring down rates for other senior contractors if I were to accept. It's worthwhile to buy a book on negotiation or do some research on the web so you will be prepared to negotiate the best rate you can.

Conclusion

Working in the SAP world can be rewarding both financially and intellectually. There are always new things to learn, new people to meet, and new projects to work on. I hope that by reading this book you've learned some tactics that will help you gain a foothold in your SAP career, and some pointers that will help take you to the next level in your SAP journey. Join the conversation and search for that next job at **AllSAPJobs.com.**

John von Aspen
Newport Beach, California

Appendix

Glossary and SAP Terminology
SAP Product glossary
http://help.sap.com/saphelp_glossary/en/index.htm
SAP Terminology lookup http://sapterm.com/
SAP Terms (humorous) http://www.asugnews.com/article/a-beginners-guide-to-sapanese

SAP Product functionality
Product Help Help.sap.com
SAP Community Network (SCN) http://scn.sap.com/welcome
SAP Support Service.sap.com

SAP Training Systems and Certification
Practice Systems and Online training
http://www.michaelmanagement.com/
Certification https://training.sap.com/shop/learninghub
Free training courses http://scn.sap.com/docs/DOC-51591

Rates/Salary Info
Computer World Survey
http://www.computerworld.com/s/article/9241548/Here_s_the_data_on_pay_perks_gender_and_visas_of_SAP_workers
SAP Salaries http://www.glassdoor.com/Salary/SAP-Salaries-E10471.htm
SAP Contracting Rates http://www.allsapjobs.com/sap-job-trends/

SAP Communities
LinkedIn Groups - SAP Community, ASUG (Local Chapter),
SAP Jobs, and more LinkedIn.com
America SAP User Group (ASUG) ASUG.com
SAP Community Network SCN.SAP.com

SAP Career Info
Tips http://scn.sap.com/community/career-
center/blog/2012/06/19/sap-career-blog-links
SAP Career Blog AllSapJobs.com/blog

Job Sites (US)
SAP Job Aggregator AllSapJobs.com
SAP Contract and Perm Positions Dice.com
Jobs at SAP CareersatSap.com
Jobs at Consulting firms/Big 4, etc. Monster.com

SAP Customers
SapCustomerList.com Includes list of thousands of companies
running SAP
Customer List Dated but still relevant

SAP Partners (Software and Consulting Services)
http://www.sap.com/partners/overview/find.html
http://global.sap.com/partners/directories/searchpartner.epx
The "Big 4" - Accenture, Cap Gemini, Deloitte Consulting, IBM
SAP Consulting

SAP Industry Solutions

SAP has different core software for some industries which require specialized skill sets and industry knowledge. People with skills in these areas can sometimes command higher rates, and these can be good focus areas for people with business experience in a specific industry.

IS-Retail
IS-Apparel and Footwear
IS-Aerospace and Defense
IS-Utilities
IS-Media
IS-Mining
IC-Mill Products
IS-Oil & Gas
IS-Chemicals
IS-Banking.
IS-Industrial Machinery and Components
IS-Software

SAP INFO

THE HUB IS INDIA!!

WHAT IS THE BEST ONLINE TRAINING FOR SAP? ANSWER FROM QUORA

1. SAP GLOBE
   011+91 733737-6600

2. TECHNOPAO

3. SAP TECH IT

4. INFOTECH

#5. SAP VITS.com
   INFO@SapViTs.com

IDES SERVICE (THE BEST)
$70 180 DAYS
SAP IDES ECC6 (EHP7 180)
MODULES. FI, CO, LE, MM, PP, QM,
PM, PS, AND SD ARE PRESENT.
(ERPTRAININGTECH.COM)